GLIMPSE OF INSPIRATION

GLIMPSE OF INSPIRATION

Jagram Singh

GenNext Publication

Published by

GenNext Publication
5, Ansari Road
New Delhi-110002

Distribution Network
gyanbooks.com
India, USA, Canada, UK, Australia, France

ISBN: 978-93-5324-181-0 (PB)

15 impression 2019

Printed at: Goyal Offset Printers, Delhi.

Blessing

'Glimpse of Inspiration'

A glimpse of inspiration is a motivating instinct, which along with expressing the maturity of mutual relationship between individual, nature and divinity in this collection of poetry compose in motion has also expresses soulful attachment in relation to nature such as elixir bathed expression, thought, words and which appears to be playing the lead role in pursuing the path of human welfare. Therefore, it would be seen as an extremely lovely and respectful instinct for all in future.

I wish him my infinite greeting for his Glimpse of Inspiration and I do also congratulate the Publisher for publishing this excellent poetry.

Best Regards

Padmashree Dr Sunil Jugi

Prologue

'Glimpse of Inspiration'

Nothing inspires more than a set of words woven together as rhymes, stories or the other forms of literature. Poetry, Stories have been the key source of inspiration for generations and it will continue to tickle the human emotions till mankind exists. The writer of the book Mr Jagram Ji himself is a man of principles. Being a 'Swayam Sevak' RSS Karykarta his devotion to the Mother Land 'Bharat Mata' and humanity itself is an inspiring experince for the people around. Devotion, Dedication, Inspiration aren't mere words for Mr Jagram Ji but he practices all that practically. His devotion to his work (Karma) and duties (Kartavya) speaks. I think the experience of his life inspired him to write this novel book. Poems and sayings of our great Saints, Poets, Philosophers have always been an inspiring force for civilization for generation. Poetry or the literature changes the direction of life when one experiences hopelessness and darkness. A poem pushes one beyond the boundaries when faced with fear. Whole world is a reflection of our thoughts and emotions which make us feel or work accordingly. A set of words inspires the nation and wins wars. New styles of writing poetry have evolved in the last decades, but the only thing that remains intact is the spirit to touch lives. The thoughts in this book are going to resonate with you deeply. This book will guide the readers to introsoect and give the hope in times of despair. The book 'Glimpses Of

Inspiration' contains a matter that will reinforce your belief in humanity and melt your heart. The writer Mr Jagram Ji deserves appreciation for writing such a good thought provoking book. Motivational word guide us to think and decide the purpose of life. I hope the readers will be inspired and enjoy the book thoroughly.

गजेन्द्र सोलंकी
(कवि)

Contents

"Obeisance to Goddess of knowledge"

O! My reverend Saraswati mother,
having pleased give pith treasure.

Give up own stage wipe the dark,
scratch night intellect lamp spark.

Spread splendour tent climbing on swan,
establish honey world in lap own.

Playing on guitar awake brains tendril,
shaking sweet tune vanish dark rill.

O! pile of intellect give boon of talent,
destroyer of ignorance fill with silent.

Taking light lamp kindle inter lamp,
fill sap of rose in darkend camp.

O! mother fill rill of inspiration,
cremating devil rise sun over creation.

"Salutation to motherland"

O! attractive sacred motherland,
assign thy immense hand.

Himalaya ornamented on forehead,
aspect of vanity adorned in blue land.

Wreath of rivers in thy neck,
White silvern Ganga in all check.

Leap spring constant in heart,
Pleasant dye echo in part.

Vindhya's belt decorated in hip,
Be ashame world mountainy strip

Sea waves as anklet bells,
Sound all parts by hollow shells

Universe portrait of quiet humanity,
Own world brotherhood's dignity,

O! fire creator motherland,
Grow sleepy seed in heart land,

O! affectionate mother allow self respect,
O! gem of treasure give un-exhaustive aspect.

"New year"

O! kinsman gin like morn rose,
whet thorny in thick bunch,
lily's lips in gay much,
in cool scented waves of wind,
honey wings in mouth bind,
dance ever shy veil lose,
O! kinsman gin like morn rose.

Sweet life as newly leaf,
be patriot as ears to deaf.
vital necklace on heart of bliss,
success saluting conveyed kiss.
be cheerful as heaven nose,
O! kinsman gin like morn rose.

"Brave soldier"

We are brave soldier,
it is mine land.

In all its varying situations
it is mine ancient sound.

Several kinsman in selfish,
liberty dream, what kind?

"Golden land Bharat"

How alike snow it shined,
White fames hands quiet kind.

All the world repeat flow
Zenith glorious greatness O! Bharat.

Ginned dawn scattered sunny,
Adorned with cream of honey.

All natural smooth parts smiled,
Shy face lovely O! Bharat.

Zephyr kissed the pink cheeks,
Golden round peeped quicks.

Lovers army attacked over youth,
Sleepy lion roared O! Bharat.

All reverend world's crown,
Day and night as fine gown.

Ram – Krishna's holy land,
Sacred lovely, remarkable O! Bharat

"Dear Bharat"

Fame thy play on high,
Cloudy force on windy sigh

Round on nature's green garden,
By step blowing bright golden.

Bias from Vedas to sacrifices,
Icy sparked by dawn tries.

Ganga landed on heart of fields,
Wrap wrapper of immortal shields.

Mountany top as calm as land,
Forest smiled as windy extend.

Rivers flew as nectar's way,
From thy day heaven away.

Ram wandered on rough chart,
Krishna played on pipe on thy heart.

Blew cool calm scented wind,
Blind world lighted by thy mind.

"Sing again Anthem"

O! Brave youth of reverend motherland,
O! Fire hands of pious sun sand.
On calls of age roared comose,
Once sing National Anthem dear.

Detect, who asides Goddess's veil,
Look, who robs lily's smell,
Preserve innocent glorious age,
Sing Anthem skilled vigiler,

Now became bleedy in tight,
Today set sacred shy sight.
Do face getting again slug,
Sing again tone clear,

A firm desire of patriotism, where lost?
Caught in cold hand ancient past,
O! Lull grow to nurture union's plant,
Sing hearty hath no fear.

"O! My Motherland"

O! My motherland,
    Thou hast grandest face.
Seeing thy beauty,
    Ashamed world's race.
Obtaining depth water,
    The sea rains calm ever,
Stable Himalaya standing to heaven,
    Steady serving deliver,
Spring coming in pious bottom,
    Dedicate thy gift.
Thy single dust drop,
    Teach honour swift.
Always goddess hath defeated,
    To tell thy fame.
In comparison of thy face,
    Garun's pace be lame,
Collseentful wind's gust,
    Come from heaven,
O! Holy land joy of thy light,
    Ray carry as raven,
Black cloud with suit,
    Having roared come again,
O! Endless destiny in thy tender feet
    Flow grave drain.
Thy sacred grove with nectar,
    Whose doth not charm,
Mode of religious songs
    Sing by cuckoo all over the farm.
Krishna told Gita's Mantras,
    Coming in thy lap.

O! Mother in thy lap,
    Flow first cultural sap.
Now having presented,
    God smiles heaven grove
O! Mother gratefulness
    My thin hairs will prove.

"A fruitful Plant"

Not a home,
    Of playing and leaping.
Not a theatre,
    Of dancing and piping.
It is a plant,
    Laden with sweety manners,
A plant of patriotism,
    Grows in heart,
Preaches to quench,
    Of faded desert,
It is a perfumes of Arabia,
    Over world's head scatter.

"Sleepy Plant"

O! Sleepy plant early awake,
    Taking rocket hand comes out.
Cruel foe robbing golden life.
    Today bearer lamenting shout.
Flame's mail wear grind the wretch,
    Sorrow's lamp's carrier put out.

"Be Diligent"

O! Dearly grove'skidden,
    Always be diligent.
No hopeless in fruitless,
    Climb up constant.
Gin like ceaseless rill,
    Gain a content.
Untired ever go ahead,
    Secure truth pleasant.

"Ode on birds of open sky"

Independent of horizon,
    Shan't sing caught in cage.
Fearlessly staggered in fire sticker,
    Gladdest wings will quite damage,
About to drink founting water,
    Shall die in hungry & thirsty.
Sour fruits better than.
    In golden bowl's sweet tasty
In tie of lustring golden,
    Absent thy free flight pace.
Now gazing in free dream,
    On tops tree's round face.
So ideas had in heart,
    Fly to touch blue farm,
Disclose mouth as red rays,
    Skylark swallow grapes warm
By prejudice of these wings,
    Aside aspect from the sky.
Either it falls in woo,
    or draw sting breath dry,
No allot shelter of nest,
    And spread in piece of twig,
But if assign strong wings,
    Then no disturb in flight big.

"Ode on village beauty"

Soft sweety green,
    Scattered a long area.
White silvern roof
    Wrapped in sunny idea,
On smooth green boldly,
    Bleeding as morn sun,
Bent on dark land
    Blue sky's fine gun.
Hand appears charmful,
    By weeds ladden corn.
Golden flowers, leaves
    And beds newly born.
Blown honey scent,
    By mustard's yellow flowers.
Peepout green land
    As night's blind followers.
Silvern golden flowers,
    Adorned mango row.
Aside tearing veil,
    Nightingale danced now,
Numberless delicious fruits,
    Born in mouth of weeds.
Comfortable shade and shelter,
    Magic fruit of its seeds.
On small plants of grove,
    Newly gin in glad.
Snow as pearl corn,
    Dance clad in mad.
The world vanish in morn,
    When sky land on soil.

The mist then loved all,
    As ocean's lap boil,
Marked on sandy rasp,
    Ganga's silvern bank.
On shore of melon's crops,
    Lay as nectar's tank.
Under blue horizon,
    Open lawn as hollow.
Unique uncommon as heaven,
    Usurp by its glow.

"Dark"

Sun and moon quite dirty,
    Quenched all of star
Today wind became poisoness,
    Salty rivers clean water,
The birds hath left voice,
    Also cattle hath no aid,
Fork as accasia on all of trees,
    Whole body seived and dead.
Perfumes of soil vanished,
    Crops suffer from fog.
Darkened waves all around,
    World appears as deserted slug.
In such way to do something,
    True and affirm duty.
I shall be a ray of nation,
    Aside all gifts of dark cruel dirty.

"Rain Queen"

Rain came again tipatips,
How! Joys brought its lips.

Will feel rest much,
Mother's lair will go such,
Numberless festivals will touch,
When it comes the green peeps.

Delicious fruits will eaten taste,
Sweetest songs will sing in heartest,
Rain! Will come again haste,
How! Blith will bring its drop creeps.

"Great Nation"

From ancient era,
Being vast and great,
By symbol of glory,
Being glorious portrait,
Drops of dense red,
Always wet battle field,
Where so nation slave,
When every lions smiled,
Where put out life lamp,
Of grateful martyrs of nation.
Flow blood like rivers
Presented every life passion.
When can absent the truth,
Filled with dedications.
Who can wipe drops,
Ofbravemen's actions.
Detested empire slavery,
Never be adopted,
No one line in history,
Which no clearly noted.
Don't detect who ignored,
Definition of slavery now.
Skirmishing on every steps,
Faking enthusiastic desiring maps.
Where history marked always,
With colour of bravery.
Bleedy fountain springed ever,
Of sacrificing water pury,
So it preserved by men,
Than a lot of wealth,
Unselfish, active dedicative men,
Need of Nation's good health.

"Our Duty"

Into the fresh joy,
Ready with swords;
Rising and ginning,
Unfear upto words.

Into the thick sorrow,
Never till coward.
Lamenting and feeling,
Aside in hard.

Into the midst depth,
Of sorrow and joy;
Standing and peeping,
As dawn toy.

Into the hands of death,
Dry palm tree,.
Dedicating and sacrificing,
Fears no free.

Into the fire home,
Needles of ash.
Kissing and flying,
In blue fresh.

Into the spring to autumn,
Always be dutyful.
Raining and flouring,
Patriotism in pitiful.

"Elegy on Kashmir"

The cruel charge today,
Taking spear in hand.
Truth asides from eyes,
Head displaces of Motherland.

What, it will go into pieces,
What, blood will change into water,
While tolerate disgrace of own,
While, Pandavas won't be chatter.

But also a line of endurance,
Fire rest on heart of sea.
The glory staggered now,
Ever gaze by shy pea.

Now history mark with blood,
Today irony steps on altar.
Come races of divided Bharat,
On calls for shade and shelter.

Setting rays call you,
Dying rose waits you.
Martyr's ashes invite you,
Dedicate for Nation whole of you.

Awake under open sky,
As furnace become stir.
Note on life's moment,
Sing Elegy on Kashmir.

"The way clear"

Ray of golden sun,
    For nation be care.
Taste of delicious fruit,
    For victory be dare.
Treasure of heavenly joy,
    For rest dig lair.
Work untired day night,
    For success clean hair.
Selfless sweet wishes,
    For honour lose share.
Remark always death,
    For delight wipe tear.
Constant like fountain
    For goal climb stair.
Band of unfeary bamboo,
    For unity belong pair
Selfish coward soldier,
    For dedication give up chair.
Slave's secret desires,
    For free no one fair.
No, dont's in any steps,
    For heaven no rare.
Do's while the breathe,
    For the way clear.

"S.O.M."
"Save our Motherland"

Sweety lovely of spring,
    Faded flowers want you.
Long fatty of rain,
    Unrilledrivers like you.
Lapof full Lunar,
    Deserted sky love you.
Zenith with icy grace,
    Staggered top kiss you.
Star of soul heart,
    Set sun gaze you.
Lover of night queen,
    Lamented moon look you.
Light of immortal soul,
    Slumbered waves call you.
Sound of glittering face,
    Worried morning catch you.
Noise of innocent infant,
    Bored evening tell you.
Green devotee of her dandy,
    Naked weeds touch you.
Perfumes of stable delight,
    Inanimate green awake you.
Goddess of wordly life,
    Whole nature embrace you.
Hands of joy and sorrow,
    Day and night wait you.
O Insane! mind now too,
    This fearless do you.

False guilty of cruel met,
    Get rid from prison you.
Save our motherland,
    Ornament whole parts you.
All the scent of Arabia,
    Smell her fame you.
Her light precious past
    Re-establish on heaven you.

"The Summon"

Grateful desires in heart,
    Out ungrateful cart.
Connect into part,
    From aside no smart.
Foe of blind's way,
    Mate of sluggish ray.
Renounce dreamday.
    Abandon timidity may.
Bore view of night,
    Smile red as light.
Free from idle sight,
    As sun glow right.
In dark shining fill,
    Eager plant by drill.
Health vary into rill,
    Ray live and dark kill.
Weeds belong green,
    Blue to green scene,
Fragrant on nector screen,
    Upto sky vast keen.
High boon to mountain,
    Horizontal ears maintain.
Alott glorious fountain,
    Assign to fish plantain.
Provoke to inanimate nature,
    Remark of mother's nurture.
Stormy pace till future,
    Threat by poisonous creature.
Mix juice of brotherhood,
    Taste yet union blood.

Bad into delicious good,
    Stick together being good.
Content as happy soon,
    Bright as innocent moon.
Grave as dust boon,
    Deep like sea noon.
So being good brave,
    Being queer upon death pave.
Attack like lion over knave,
    Surprise all the traitor's save.
Rootout all the heap,
    Grind deceiving creep.
Ban on steps of leap,
    So pat never peep.
On throne ban goddess,
    Whole of one now bless.
Present such immortal tress,
    Dedicate wreath of greatness.
Peace vary into rage,
    Adorn history by truth page;
Shine be sun sage,
    Raise on summo way.

"The Message"

Black portrait of blue surface,
Fast pace like boundless face,
Life clearly breathes of heart,
Spotless stars of hopeful race.

Faithful from gather in heart,
Selfless raptures fix in mind,
Ahead untired lord of pace,
No disappear in bunch of blind.

Depart kind mate of pity,
Hang bags of elegy song.
Aside boat of selfish ocean,
Adorn in heart benevolence long.

Shameful deed by cruel man,
Rootless hairs from shy head.
Disgrace drops of graceful rill,
Wipe countenance by mean lead.

Holy portrait be frail bleedy,
Harsh cruel rope linked round.
So dull whetless ornament,
By thick force area bound.

Now like helpless orphan,
Gaze way for one piece of bread.
Usurp right of golden throne,
By force rest on rough thread.

Grace of self respect forehead,
Became as waterless tank.
Cover heart by sorrow cloth,
Being moments as skelton bank.

White face round like yellow,
Green grove in lap of death today
Meaningless heap of valueless dust,
Useless skin of setting day.

Everyday burns from thunder rare,
Day moments in cage by foe,
Fainted like autumn season,
Striet ban to summer toe.

In cruel prison of vampire,
In unendurable black speed.
Struggles as out of water fish,
Breathes became hollow reed.

Thou art now life cane,
Full of you stars of night.
Kindle the life lamp of hope,
Wipe ailment of heart by joy light.

Honey hopes of mother's way
As thunderbolt of west wind.
Overwhelmed all to blossom grove,
Float on duty by sound mind.

O Ruby! Don't sleep now,
Don't dip in depth of wealth.
Come! Protect her holy veil,
Pierce spear into foe health.

O Volcano! Absent in fort of isolation,
Comose with victorious fire rage.
No rest on indolence bed now,
Hurry up on truth message.

"The Origin"

Down queen sunny mantle,
Covering herself wonders out.
Smiling paste on bed lips,
On glow mouth sweet shout.

Honey crises of mad wind,
By newly born top of leaves.
Like deep well of perfumes,
Be slave of spring's suit lives.

All the natures as new bride,
And the faces like air and fire.
Daring slights check all steps,
Glady turns free admire.

Call dearly by hand voice,
Spread waits on coming way.
Kick that who loves warm,
Be spring, desires by mind ray.

No rest detect deprive one
Morn waits between such.
Youth noise fork in hand,
Burry depth silence much.

Grave spirit of depth ocean,
High morale of zenith sky.
Patience of land sparks of stars,
Rocket in front so frank try.

Stormy garland wears in neck;
Life of youth seen on youth stage.
Tide waves as sea in heart,
In way lot of pace rage.

Glorious top like toppest Himalaya,
Glittering crown white as snow.
Blue fancy boundless ambitions,
Fearless sunny limitless vow.

Atoms in millions of fire hands,
Equitter's sun in rays of eyes.
Horror cloudy roars in creator,
Fake with expect in all dyes.

Foe of dark, O lightened glove!
Hide in cold hands of death.
Penetrable whole of impenetrable horizon,
Displant for ever darkened health.

Dream of bark autumn to spring,
Dark maid quest fate both.
Kindle lamp of long life hope,
Peep early origin! From sloth.

"Own Longing"

Rest heart of flowers,
A group of flowers;
Tongue's sweet kiss,
No for its dish.

Sweet lovely fun,
Mad green nun.
Hobby of floating,
None for nothing.

Shade of delight,
Shelter of might ,
Ray of green sprout,
Neither for spout.

Sky of bright fame,
Noise of sea tame.
Throne of heaven,
No touch of even.

O Lord! Fearless necklace,
Last moment of race.
Fast ardent of patriotism,
Never its prism.

Mighty good will,
Remark last till.
Imperishable desire,
No miss in admire.

"Ode to Anguish"

On pain as depth of soul of nation,
The exertion challenges displays.

Waiting path whole of time,
Hope of flash of time.
By stable curious mouth,
Shook the suffering rays.

Aside brakes of attraction,
Kindle the sweet stops of affection.
Rising over the blue top,
Only foe fire tide pays.

Honey tuning of dark night,
Faded lips of earth might.
Quiet tone of untired soul,
Always on icy head plays.

Raining into fire hand,
Shameful in naked band.
Sudden spiritless as corpse,
Fount being Sundays.

Marshy of golden holy land,
Clouds of abhor hand.
Like rare feary grove,
Ready snake such mislays.

Taking icy cruel stick,
Powerful wind mad thick.
Rich roaring upon limitless sky,
Straight as unshamed disarrays.

Numberless poisonous enemies,
For own mission front armies.
Staring to the boundaries,
Neatlessfoot steps lays.

Dear Gandhar caught in cage,
Healthy breathes turn the page,
By an atheist devil,
Frozen on the excrete decays.

Ancient glorious glory,
Of heaven ever green story.
Whole parts of body scented.
But now as autumn hays.

Coming out gem of Ashwashthama,
Suffered as patient of Asthama.
On heart of Dharm and the culture,
Pierced, for red strays.

Lovely in death's chain,
Dry dear deep drain.
But tongue near the teeth,
Fragle part of heart says.

Sindh such in pocket of sad,
Without oxygen no breathes glad.
Surrounding by vigour invaders,
Fight in night gays.

Insulting the pious places,
Being hell the muddy races.
Statues of god and goddess,
Into sand shape by the ways.

Plundered the treasure of 'lily',
Without honey as tasteless jelly,
In the lanes of barren area,
No shine safe stays.

Invincible emperor Sikandar,
Vanished in sun as star.
Set the ego of winning,
For new life own preys.

Lighted by unique victory,
Knitted by remarkable history.
Dedicating a lot of delicious juice,
Adorned the colourful trays.

Now lamenting soul of Ravi,
As orphan and becoming navvy.
CalmlessKinglaj and Nankana now,
Seeing hopeful saving ways.

Bleeding fount left side,
Painful sore on cuts wide.
Spread the drops of rainy clouds,
And in narrow corner sprays.

Burning like dry cheer wood,
Being so barren of babyhood.
Bored banks of died river,
O Cloud! Today heart prays.

Ancient fine uniform of east,
Filling joy in innocent breast.
Young youth of young yellowish,
Ready now own shine slays.

Dancing stage of mornings,
Joyful heart of shining.
Lap of goddess Kamakhya,
Spotless whiteness change into grays.

Left and right parts of body,
Wet by the drops of bloody.
Hide in walls of darkness of dark,
Where it is? Crowling Mays.

Great Himalaya trembling in fear,
Fearing like fountain clear.
In prison of black subordination,
To be fixed in fatal clays.

Wary guard to last of life,
Faithful follower to whet of knife;
In all the stages of season,
Like brave Laxman! Ready always.

The centre of priests pious Kailash,
'Manas pearl' in other hand's cash.
The daughter of Gangotry and Jamunotry,
Slumbers in lap of death bays.

Covered and fulfilled with wealth,
By caring of nature for good health.
Fro flow like follower of fountain,
Ahead without any fear in frays.

Temples of sages and saints,
Bank of light of life moments.
In the 'Ashok garden' to 'Mother Sita'
Something hope in nays.

Scented Kashmir as heaven,
Converted moon shape into raven.
Roaring of uncontent and noise,
Wandered free as tune of brays.

Innocent soul of martyrs,
Bleeding pipes upon stirs.
Burning like mouth of lamp,
Across the ocean by help of drays.

Bowl of wealth like an ocean,
Lovely attractive bird golden.
The swan whiteness winner,
Being stork like flays.

Forshake the sweet tune of selfish
Upon the unselfish sea swim O fish.
Foe of night mother's son,
For joy by dark betrays.

Single rays of hope in heart,
Powerful tide of beating to start.
Anguish! for golden glory of golden era,
So contented fruitful delays.

Pained caught in frail brain
So narrow dried summer drain.
Delicate lamented worried heart,
O son! BeDussehra for joys.

"Guidance"

Principleless politics,
Grinds the nation.
Foilless treasure
Nurtures corruption.

Reasonless pleasure,
Invites the atrocity.
Characterless education,
Marks the conceity.

Moralityless business,
Changes into swindler.
Humanityless science,
Reforms the butcher.

Sacrificeless worship,
Erases the culture.
Failureless success,
Turns the future.

Nectorless night,
Flows despair.
Delightless day,
Urges to cheerless lair.

Hopeless breathes,
Calls powerlessly.
Promiseless duty,
Unfolds treachery.

Merciless cruelty,
Preys humanity.
Loyaltyless fidelity,
Cremates Nationality.

Ceaseless pace,
Assigns salvation.
IntentlessOccu,
Guides to mission.

"Don't aside"

Plans from work,
Present from past.
Work from hand,
Progress from vast.

Determination from habits,
Thoughts from mind.
Crime from guilty,
Humanity from kind.

Sorrow from nights,
Delight from day,
Might from union,
Cruelty from hay.

Water from rivers,
Forest from weeds.
Plants from roots,
Desires from needs.

Moon from sky,
Clouds from wind.
Fountain from play,
Patience from blind.

Heat from fire,
Pleasure from gay.
Varity from taste,
Fairy from may.

Gods from heaven,
Silence from death.
Beauty from nature,
Wonders from wealth.

Depth from ocean,
Zenith from sky.
Magnitude from earth,
Honesty from try.

Splendour from lamp,
Pearl from shell.
Dreams from breaths,
Truth from smell.

Tears from life,
Result from hope,
Role from action,
Wishes from scope.

Rights from liberty,
Continuity from fountain.
Benevolence from foundation,
Morale from mountain.

Patriotism from patriot,
Concentration from goal.
Constancy from cruel,
Modesty from coal.

Peace from alone,
Time from pace.
Loyalty from duty,
Next from race.

"A song of spirit"

Frantic dancing again nice,
A numberless lives fully sacrifice.

Throne of glory lighted by foe heads,
Beginning destruction song push ray leads

Similarity, liberty, sailed the nation,
Every cruel waves pushed spirit motion.

The waves of funeral pipes to kiss zenith,
An admire on fire, to crave into depth.

The mouth of fork being choice part laps,
The resolution and dedication perfumed map.

Now celebrate festival with all the breathes,
Such mean evil spirit in fire hands of hearths.

Weakness of life always that cowardice,
Achievement of life always that noble voice.

The dutyfullloyality rose future ways,
The dedicative bravery lighted extinct rays.

"Recreation for Creation"

Into the deep down,
Loose upto glow.
Constant effort till,
Delicious woo flow.

Into the lily hope,
Wait up till light.
Ceaseless pleasing tone,
Warm spirit to fight.

Into the bride sound,
Fearless bid flow.
Depth and zenith gem,
Morn moan slip slow.

Into the scent sight,
Seem rill fountain.
Fragile fun need form,
Silly mute mountain.

Into the tiny dial,
Paddy more voice;
Chain till train will,
Pin drop choice.

Into the plot dish,
Perfume sweet arm.
Fishing wish time face,
Meaningless quench farm.

Into the dawndresh,
Fear tyre blund.
Rousy to race nice,
Fine bitter plund.

Into the rise gown,
Blossom matches bliss.
Barren deed dead near,
Truth alone never miss.

Into the eye pool,
Creeperless smile ray.
Blind stagger aim none
Play fresh another may.

Into the stormy night,
Steady stepping march.
Unfair speary way,
Fan teeth cease starch.

Into the trampy win,
Toe tress prime brain.
Troops on haily word,
Hellish lap drain.

Into the colour gay,
Colt desirezealtry.
Cheery spring ever grove,
Saddest tune dry.

Into the fort try,
Sweet peril joy.
Floating doubt burry,
Burry upon flute toy.

Into the ready reed,
Than there now.
Pipe on peep done,
Soul merely vow.

Into the dream plane
Greedy recent temptation.
Adorn every Recreation,
For unique sound Creation.

"Sporting Spirit"

Affirm born date,
Mortal sure mate,
Breathes miraclerate,
Trust fish late.

Sweet face moon,
Flame race noon.
Blith grace boon,
Time pace soon.

Sense chance near,
Talk sweet dear.
Tongue joy pear,
First to last clear.

Think so spring,
Chain win wing.
Perfume truth ding,
Link hammer swing.

Seek so much,
Heaven as vouch.
Heart beating touch,
Shadow mate such.

Pursue like coil,
Mix colour soil,
Fide worst boil,
Stream uncease moil.

Do's always,
Horizontal days,
Dead valley ways,
Morn golden rays.

Untire zeal rain,
Ocean kiss drain;
Grove light brain,
Miss no this train.

Ready indeed,
Will never need,
Nectar bowl seed,
Noble mission reed.

Real role being blind,
None be the wind,
Sporting spirit in mind,
How much may be kind.

"The tears of Pillars"

Collect the fair dream,
Reserve heaven to mouth.
Spread all over the world,
Twice pole north and south.

Float upon the imagine ocean,
No peril in journey, but plea.
Blind devotee mission to note,
Splendour meaningless various clea.

Clear sense all the steps,
For new fresh morn.
Zeal wearing the kite flight,
For to quite the horn.

Light guides the dancing spring,
But misguide on thick way.
Now surprize surrounding moon,
Above "icy lass" marshy day.

Wishing whole sacrifice,
Build matchless grace,
Present the dream world,
Burry into depth the nice face.

All the glitters none attract,
From the sacred soul path,
Catch no waxy neat and sweet fly,
Need no amuse than peace hath.

Hunt the joyful plane,
Entertaining colourful plays,
Amaze fully utopia's treasure,
Blow sun with gay of may.

Kiss the rousy cheeks,
Fall in immense suit never,
Pass the whole of life,
In valley of the dear.

Being the smiling toys,
In the busy lane of the fair.
Ask to the nature nurse,
What being the romantic pair.

Fight in chilly hand,
Touch time again more,
Swing against kindling lamp,
No sweeten a little honey desert of bore.

In the end to reign in hell,
Than to stave in heaven.
Fell the domestic songs,
Having no will cuckoo than raven.

Play on the sweet seed,
In the beatingless heart.
Surprize the universe,
By miracle nice part.

Flow being boundless river,
To take spice of life,
Never worry from variety,
Hope tan nothing as whet in knife.

Many flowers selection dream,
Holy grove scent in the sun.
Avoid the luxurious flight,
Banish being monk and nun.

The power land on the stage,
Dance against being snakes.
Tremble the history then,
Fine hands like sword put out quakes.

Play the best role,
On this noble stage.
But wrong running fruit,
Expressed unspiritualpage by sage.

Found the toppest reward,
On fork mouth of nature race.
Move around across the horizon,
Being iron chariot future pace.

Now fall ill in will,
Wash spot from the silk.
No patience stand in arm,
As whiteness without milk.

Pass the journey for new,
How much gain in bag.
Something rest on the bank,
A drop enough in range of tag.

Dwell in sky under the shade,
Joint relation show the best.
Collect for man have no desire,
Serve the life for another test.

Give up the chance of joy,
As like morn to even.
Freeze the ocean of boy,
In the bowl of stage of seven.

The dragon earth around,
Against exist on the hair.
And the universal universe,
Bossom in heart of darkend lair.

None care for willing cure,
Pat no someone in the rain.
Shelterless the birds without next,
What safe place in the drain.

Forget the straight way,
Present in feet of waves.
Surely to nurture in temple,
But to switch willing in the caves.

Lose the precious breathes,
In the darkened bottom of river;
So much open the coneh,
Worry without boredom clever.

In the stream land,
Slumber the prime night owl.
Above the dawn freedom,
Fain in dead cruel howl.

The grandest place on the chest,
For the miracle glory.
The flower of fame like sun,
Establish on the heaven this story.

A single drop of blood
Never saved for own might
In search of lotus feet,
Over the worship with all sight.

O! the pain served all on fact,
Again rejoiced in spring leaves.
But today icy to prey,
Through messenger garland is weaves.

Unfurle the cracks of miles,
Shoot how much shoot.
Conceal the sweat tone,
Get rid from the heal of boot.

Slope of flow wings,
Wear narrow red right.
Make up as the vampire,
Abhor magic unique light.

Autumn smile to sow,
On several the purple lamp.
Switch on the whole energy,
But nobody illuminated the camp.

Remain in other hand,
Lead personality royal.
In certain new bride's parts,
Best facility loyal.

Don't spite on the whiteness,
Forgetting O! Kinsman once.
Reality same return behind,
Mud of thunder offence.

Sorry, it down so,
That gurgle the foam please;
Queer method scratch dumb,
In rare rite seem cheese.

Fight in sour hand,
Round in glowing glove.
Pierce into hairy side,
Choose best innocent dove.

Being ask to the martyr
Brush quietly detested spot.
Tuning of sorrow hammer,
Endure loudly regarding a lot.

As no victory of zealousy,
Although sound of busy bees.
So much no wonder of patience,
In the consciousness of the trees.

Without care stand upto date,
Without lamentation swing into fly.
Without spare perfumes of beginning,
Between the stairs took of sky.

The new generation so and so,
Never avoid this stage.
Being blunder piece into piece
Noise allow against the image.

Lonely preach of sacred drop,
Into the link in dynamic chain.
The holy river of defence and glory,
Stood alike unfeared the rain.

But today swifty handsome,
Varied the whole of taste into sour.
Naked the portrait laden with gem,
Count in the cage within pour.

O! piece of vision peep alike sun,
Always smile in tight and fight.
O! ray of mission sight into nun,
Recent quick same in right and might.

No, legend it such form of truth,
Floor the ancient river of the tears of pillars.
In a hazard day around the butter blith,
At the bank of sand as delta similar.

"My Mother"

The Himalaya is crown,
And Ganga is Mother.
All of the top that;
Bharat, no another.

Chitrakoot is holy land,
And Shri Ram is flow.
Arjun is patience,
Krishna is revered vow.

Holy preach of Kurukshetra,
Gita is the way.
Meera, Tulsi, Soor, Kabir,
Devotee songs always.

Truth, steal nonviolence,
Pure heart everyday.
Only life for good work,
Fruitless sweat play.

This is place of culture,
For all the welfare,
After too variety same,
One of the more care.

A farm of scent,
Very cool and fresh.
Nature ready to welcome,
Mother! So revered and flash.

Doth piled unjustice,
On thee by another.
Noted on wind water,
Sand delete for ever.

But try little good,
By drop no sever.
Sticked on depth,
Dead dream, but never.

"Life is ice"

Life is ice dream,
Every may marked;
Unfear into grief,
May mighty parked.

Greatly march for sure,
Tiny doubt never.
Unto thee such pure,
Truly upto ever.

"Dear innocent rest"

A moment impossible,
    Without them.
Peaceful and real,
    Without such gem.

As cloudy unlucky,
    Without such water.
As might saddy-maddy,
    Without nice flotter.

The waves are joy of sea,
    Appears always.
Tide way of new born,
    Praising all days.

Sweat bunch of wind,
    Pierced into holes.
Clay sweaty embracing,
    Revered juicy soles.

Sound stable lap,
    Wonder heartedly song.
Constant resound pure,
    Priest play long.

Breathless way zero,
    Lamy hope in depth,
No doing no goal,
    Patience only truth.

Waterless edge sure,
    Fish pledge fail.
Only fighting in war,
    As shore on sail.

Bless desire fully,
    Life that is best.
Thou lap only now
    Dear innocent rest.

"Take from all"

Take from all,
It no but.
Boat on shore,
Hand no hut.

Constant waving,
Roaring pace.
Old influence,
O result grace.

Depth on sea heart,
Control naturally.
Ever will of point,
Horizon surely.

Dream beauty icy,
Heartedly embrace.
Tide of utopia,
Luckly trace.

Respect of the soul,
Wonderful way.
Global such good,
Whole irony day.

First of the bridge,
Stone in that.
So a sacrifice same,
Recent scent that.

Fluent of blood,
Untirely will.
Stability of breath,
Sturdy mere rill.

Unique way of firm,
Inner power.
Uncomparable afford,
Undie cap shower.

Break of the breathing,
Never borny new
On the last of tour,
Never rest sew.

Into the onetime,
And again chance.
Please hands on head,
Nothing next dance.

How will aside"

How will aside,
Because be breath,
Without no more time,
Perhaps become death.

Take all of sum,
Surely pay delightly.
Agree upto whole,
Never back lightly.

Steering of the joy,
Simply hand over.
No little lament,
Whole blith take over.

Whether may be please,
Inspite of admire.
Obedient till last,
Kindling lamp tire.

Into the suspicious dark;
Be nectarly drop.
Fatal waves of ocean,
Be untirely crop.

Thus sailing too shut,
Across safely way.
Aid to oath always,
Constant 'sun' day.

Fruit cause so much,
Soul like gem such.
Into the darkened path,
Lonely endless lamp much.

A little of doing,
If into rest last
Possible to please new,
Specially aim vast.

On dream no another,
Accepted all the same.
Willing to shade & Shelter,
Continue in heart fame.

"Merged into breath"

Merged into breath,
Being lime pace.
Disclosed above earth,
Being fine face.

Cloudily waves around,
Being sweat shower.
Thick dark creeper,
Being sweep blower.

Into the thorny mouth,
Being deep joy.
Dead shoares engage,
Being new hands toy.

Dense sorrow lighted,
Having done smiling
Autumn into granary,
Having dropped kissing.

Totally desert heart,
Being filled past.
Dried whole some weeds,
Being blissed hast.

Sudden rain laugh,
Being really happy
Feary fully boon,
Being fallen swampy.

Safe done last will,
Being more than more.
Fully black shelter,
Being aside core.

Done of whole sum,
Being alike dust.
Illusion totally far away,
Being past glass must.

Lonely wish risk,
Being into enter.
Little of life only,
Being affirm one centre.

"Whole of present"

Whole of present,
Welcome most,
Whole of pay,
Will done post.

Tour on the duty way,
As long as easy,
Lamp on the constant,
Naturally busy.

Sweat play first,
Hand over sole.
Fairy joy thirst,
Milestone pole.

Front of glassy now,
Surrendered really,
Against last ash,
Mission won fully.

Little drop of blood,
Over all done.
Fastly ready sure,
Unlimited into tone.

Fountaining show of all,
Handless tasty fruit.
Constant working role,
Now may impossible tuit.

First of fast flow,
Powerless worldly game,
Huge depth surely sum,
Untire some zeal flame.

Pray for humbly ocean,
Specially at last rest.
Pretty surprise toys,
Wrapping queer zest.

"Now never rest"

Now never rest,
Scent of grove,
Sweatly no of way,
Inner of dove.

Lost of whole,
None suspect few.
Affirm constant dove,
Faith dear dew.

Simply devotion of all,
Clear pace on motive
Hastily serially stable,
Sense of fluently active.

Fast wordly motion,
Inspiration of do's sure,
Disclosely pray of day,
Awareness of downpure.

Handover fruitly,
Recently delicious end.
Dusting embrassupto,
Justification till present.

Well come bore actually,
Identity of whole dust.
Meaningless glitterous way,
Morn suspect into lust.

Whole into sacred mouth,
As river into vast sea.
Nectarous peace and then,
When inner constant plea.

"By the new present"

By the new present,
Will be become gold,
By the new steps,
Will be gained gold.

At the last steps,
New spread all over.
And revived again,
With the new cover.

Selfly dead breathe
Smile with flow
All over perfumes free,
And beware dead slow.

Into fear dream,
Smile and be fruitful,
Wonder! Maintained zero
Finally lost lawful.

In the breathing way,
Surely constant try,
Whole of thorny path,
Easy solved the cry.

Into the hands,
Morn to welcome mist,
Yester night today,
Ready as spy lost.

Hand over yourself,
Embraced into light.
Free from the such duty,
Now only formal fight.

"Now will be free"

Now will be free,
From this sea.
Goal will be gain,
From this plea.

Flow regain to camp,
Constant being breath,
Hand helped to work,
Being powerful health.

Aside dark urgent,
From way to good new.
Friendly seat reflection,
Endstart just few.

Fast pace of flow,
Scientifically nectarous,
Clear guide to role,
Priest sure precious.

Journey with fearlessly,
Become completely free.
In all cases regularly pace
Fruitful such tree.

Constant attempt lonely,
Scentful golden time.
Silent with itself,
Sure as clear time.

Result sure possible,
Only way of sacrifice.
Boundless fresh present,
Only next new voice.

Goal comes to door

Goal comes to door,
With long life.
Way become near,
With sweat wife.

Tear by worst curse;
Ash truly strange,
Into prison of unknown,
Down such fine range.

Miss the way in ego,
Truth into the dust.
When fork sting on;
Spear to soul must.

In the glitters home,
Lost whole stress.
Sudden onto dew pace;
Surrender aside press

Tiny wish to final,
But try best darely,
Promise to fruit easy,
No hesitation clearly.

Hand over to goal,
Hope light only soul.
Whole devotion to truth,
As in the lap, pearl.

Problems itself solved,
Only the way of touch.
Free from the siny tie,
Near the good time such.

Disclosed the lucky day,
Unfilly eager to fill.
Chance sefly to come,
Now way become rill.

And now no wish

And now no wish,
Boat to the bank.
Become clear waiting,
Night fear so blank.

Whole of wish completed,
As quiet rejoy play.
Totally demand stick,
To be refill next day.

Effort in the dark,
Regain new hand.
Running on the spear,
New borny smile band.

Boundless longing sound,
Free from the system.
Sorrowful unlime face,
Asiding from gem.

Constant hope gaze,
Only drop is sufficient.
Havock desire of lusting,
Completely dum and silent.

If impossible become possible,
Holy heaven like dust.
All of the dwarfs feeling,
Having zeal inner past.

As like so that gain,
Content priest set down.
Only content in rest,
By luckly boon of crown.

If there is constant pace;
And devotion for work.
Then still no one remark,
None vacant place of fork.

Now bell has gone

Now bell has gone,
And none of the rest.
All perfumes will ready,
No one be fall next.

As an stick for the came,
And bosom friend to you.
Goal also ready beneath,
Stop, because near by you.

Fresh uniform to ruine,
Good wish to new zeal.
Breaking breath revived,
Self devotion for the real.

Tire some way help;
Hopeless to free circulation.
Stability of appointed lamp,
Best flow of determination.

Wholly land to be shine,
Heartedly tide well done.
All the secret will disclose;
Eager to endless tone.

Dumb speaks clearly,
Woo of way very easily.
Tongue surprised with joy,
Silent path change to busy.

Gazzing just point more,
Steering itself tanless.
Busy into dense wrath,
Overwhelmed for the guess.

A drop into the oceans,
Felt pleasure so more.
Such dream frank to do,
Also having done bore.

Finally so on fruit

Finally so on fruit,
In the end of way.
Having gone fill,
Inner dark away.

Black shade tears,
With pity for new.
Rainy to be showered,
Having fast done few.

Rilling on the road,
Being tide of joy.
With best present,
Scented neck toy.

Faded all smile,
Only kissing touch
Spread all over
So effective much.

Sin also changed
With nectarous play.
Cap of lovely wish,
Beware into the day.

Silent way full filled,
With heavenly delight.
In all the way of show,
Kindled tiny having fight.

That has gone shine,
All breathes be possed.
Work has done content
Luckly river accrossed.

Fruit always to real,
If attempts way pure.
And then will remain
Victory behind sure.

Now again the way

Now again the way,
With any doubt.
Long desire today,
Taken sweat fruit.

Against this help,
Sure on the top.
On this edge,
Will be sent mop.

Having take help;
Start to journey.
Only under this
Creation honey.

Regular inspiration
will become patience,
Continue working,
For lamp influence.

Actually path sweaten,
But feeling best.
Only wish mission.
Attempt with rest.

Work as for nectar,
Very delicious taste.
Into the dead heart,
Sweaten next haste.

Fruit of the work,
Last of wish,
Scarifies solely way,
Of new tasty dish.

But nobody next,
For such waiting.
And no one current,
For clear rating.

Drop to the ocean,
Complete dedication.
Then after be sure;
Goal with cremation.

What had I wanted

What had I wanted,
All the gain in hand.
Time also had passed,
All the will to land.

Fruits of hard efforts,
As like so had gotten,
Whole of the desire,
Content for good heaven.

Sudden all into pocket,
Free from the all.
Unlighted lamp lighted,
After then dark fall.
Internally waves of joy,
But cannot be expressed.
So position as dumb,
Since in sea tide forced.

Faith in their attempt,
Work welcome most.
Dead heart also ready,
Every where sorrow lost.

Success also surrendered,
Against the hard work.
Very heartedly presented,
All their sweat mark.

Very good friend's hand,
Loudly rejoice much.
Boat with shade for solutions,
All over the lot such.

Sun of lot out of blame;
Influence of dark to aside.
A little hand only way,
Rill full filled, Blank hide.

If in the heart faith,
All possible in world.
If in heart promised to dedicate,
Sure blithe beneath no word.

How it will pass

How it will pass,
In the scent of grove.
Heavenly joy again,
Into flowery love.

Lightened on high,
Noise of in fant,
Sleepy so surprise;
With loud of chant.

Dew to ready,
With sure fortune.
All is tooeager,
Surrender with tune.

Fan shy showed,
Lost of you,
Sudden to over take,
Finally till you.

No there gazing
Tears of the pair.
So guideless way,
Miss own lair.

Senseless feeling
Totally absentness.
Aside from next,
Internally lifeless.

Drops has no reply,
So eager to play.
But continue to pray,
For pleasure may.

In hands of sweat,
But no fill up full,
As may be mad woo,
But no feary lull.

If that is follower,
Then after no freedom.
If work solved,
Sure near to kingdom.

Life is meaningless,
With our sweat scent.
If that is no fire,
Otherwise whole blunt.

Lonely passing wish,
Hands with toys.
Spring will be long;
Birth on earth always.

Face like sweat

Face like sweat,
Base of play,
Life like new
Waves of day.

In the dark
Switch on.
Dead lap,
With son.

Step by step
Great joy.
Under the feet
Feeling try.

Muddy path
Softy mouth.
Fly of dream
Neither south.

Leafless lands
Again smile.
But sorrow
Happy as pile.

Lap of spring,
Delicious taste,
New circulation
So busy haste.

Hair to mouth
High tide only,
Seem sure
Present holy.

Light of fire,
Zeal of whole.
But sweaty kiss,
Fresh on pole.

Scent of beauty,
Kill of pure.
Embrace is rest
Showers now cure.

Aside from set,
Hear to last.
Aside from curse
Near to vast.

May be so possible,
When thy hands.
Ready to fire,
Lastly bands.

Heaven also under

Heaven also under,
Only by dawn.
Being fresh wonder,
Whole has flown down.

Hands in that,
That is strange.
Fruit so chance,
That is arrange.

Stopped the tears,
Having scene such.
Tired the feet,
Fire against much.

Into spider home,
Confused totally.
Up and down dumb,
Faint so actually.

Fruits of age,
Joy of day.
Cloud as shade,
Sweater now lay.

Bliss on heart,
New born free.
Sweatly embrace,
No tension as tree.

In cap of dawn,
Born hurry may.
Dream under depth,
That will being play.

So high attachment,
Now on the blood.
Slave became to dust,
Aspecting so flood.

Way will be passed,
Always on busy.
Freedom will be sure,
Moment with easy.

That is holy stream,
Revered of flow.
Breathing as whole,
End of zenith glow.

Fruit of ant

Fruit of ant,
Now born,
Fast of fake;
Show adorn.

That was waited,
Fine face.
That was hoped,
Fruitful race.

Only for flame
Ready sight.
Only for tame,
Then might.

Wish of way,
With him.
So same more,
On swim.

Beauty on leg,
But on near.
Gradually blow,
All ross spear.

Shore at last,
With handful.
Solely lean stick,
Of cheerful.

Effort constant,
Days lost.
Hurry to worry,
As river to coast.

Really will come,
What! That at think.
All the switch on,
That was link.

Speared the heart;
Come out clear.
Waiting the goal,
Shaddy so dear.

Fulfilled the pot,
Only the wish.
Boating to stick,
Rest as fish.

Possible by work,
All the best.
Good day must;
Completely rest.

All is the work,
Good will come.
Regularity of priest,
God lost some.

When will come from east

When will come from east,
Being fearful threat.
The cloud will hide in next,
Then and there to beat.

And out of from the blue,
As powerful raid.
Shad will aside sudden,
Take up, using maid.

When will attack will hammer,
By cause of hate.
Then fall in all totally,
Having without gate.

Dead waves of feary cloud,
Hand over into war.
All the black in shaped,
Will be set as morn star.

Cruel pace of west wind,
Influence will lose.
Thorny stops so many,
All the stress will comose.

Terrory face into prison,
None with you today.
In irony hands, won't pass
Within swampy bay.

Hopes of the stingless,
Fastly merged into earth.
Wishing of roaring tide,
In the mouth of heart.

Who will see you then,
And who will collect.
No one be rest of,
At that again connect.

Why are you playing in blood,
Only for handful grain.
Whom for this golden home,
By another's main.

All the collection will be here,
Only point of money.
Continuously always will feel,
And again sweat of honey.

For another become Ganga,
Regularly kindle like lamp;
All of the nature, embrace,
As emotional pillar of camp.

For the actives of whole,
Any you are, this is pure way.
Everyday having take-up own,
Revive for future depends on gay.

There is no sore

There is no sore,
And no any burn.
There is no curse,
And no any turn.

There is no sin,
And no any sorrow.
There is no burden,
And no any follow.

There is no world,
And no any sad.
There is no hollow,
And no any mad.

There is no tears,
And no any formality.
There is no spear,
An no any casualty.

There is no more,
And no any roar.
There is no attach
And no any abhor.

There is no fork,
And no any fault.
There is no plot,
And no any hault.

There is no un-justice,
And no any lead.
There is no appetite,
And no any dead.

That is my home,
There is nectar.
That is my cap,
There is actor.

That is my soul,
There is bone.
That is my ooze,
There is fresh grone.

That is my duty
There is affirm.
That is my beauty
There is confirm.

That is my nest;
There is shelter.
That is my rest,
There is center.

If a little dust
Adorn on my head.
Therefore this chance
Passed in first for ahead.

Revenge upto result

Revenge upto result,
Cruel flame uptoash.
Rest no chance also,
Surely peace dash.

Across the border
Rules be come silent.
And relation also missed,
Violence way now present.

Behind all the escape,
Possibility out of drain.
Decision has taken top,
Internally refused brain.

Now same will occurred,
That will in battle.
Rest without any fear,
As free and a gap cattle.

So much in fate,
Will be present.
Who has flowers,
Sure fruitly scent.

Not only a moment,
At a time all the clear.
Dark in the morn,
Swiftly on the spear.

In the prison of day,
Only lamentation's sound.
And then own working,
Fear will be shaking loud.

I know perfect all,
Only way of fire.
In front of complete dumb,
But fully silent admire.

The peace wants blood,
Last of talking never.
It will possible on funeral,
Because cost all for ever.

After war will take a galp,
Or death will order to stop.
On the pile so much joy,
And stop the next mop.

Finally will being shelter,
For the next will take poison.
Embrace all the nature,
Spring in autumn mission.

No chance more

No chance more;
Upto set.
No dance more,
Joy of pet.

Now we affirm,
Taking oath.
In the battle,
Against both.

Into the sword;
Sound of win.
For the mission,
Ahead no sin.

Steps no entry,
Failed totally.
Surely fear lost,
Patience actually.

Blood of flood,
All over.
A pile of more,
Tops too cover.

Constant fighting,
As long as rest.
Lighted till last,
For the best.

Wait for sound,
And nothing.
Completely tire,
But zest something.

And then loud of,
In the blues.
Embrace of sea,
Solved aim true.

Only wating so much,
For this.
Against bravely,
But irony no miss.

River found sea,
Blithe at last.
Ready to never,
Please fast.

What so possible
Convey that.
For asiding of dark;
Light as fast.

Saying this boldly,
Into the west.
Totally sink down,
Into blue nest.

After dying too,
Appear again.
For new dream,
Light rain.

Light as lamp,
Constant on door,
Ready for present,
Not only poor.

Bell has gone

Bell has gone
Ready to fire.
Light has done,
Stepsup no tire.

When the sun arised,
Dark behind haste.
When the new heard,
Breathe stick as paste.

Hope became flash,
And all into dust.
Before the sun,
Caught in lust.

Now only rest,
Will be remain.
When it will pass,
Know god brain.

What you did
That fruit sure.
As you sow in it,
Result always pure.

Decide and ready,
Crops in hands,
In the last so must,
Fruit in bands.

Suddenly clouds over,
Nothing so same.
In a single moment,
Dogs and cats glow flame.

Before which was
Now in tears.
That was in the sky,
Today on the spears.

Totally dark shamed,
Confusion solved.
New face in the east,
Then possibility proved.

Victory into legal,
Lamps on the way.
Newly confidence,
Rejoice on the play.

Certainty is truth,
Breathing of active.
Basically that is facts,
Current so for motive.